797,885 Books
are available to read at

Forgotten Books

www.ForgottenBooks.com

Forgotten Books' App
Available for mobile, tablet & eReader

ISBN 978-1-333-79627-3
PIBN 10553370

This book is a reproduction of an important historical work. Forgotten Books uses state-of-the-art technology to digitally reconstruct the work, preserving the original format whilst repairing imperfections present in the aged copy. In rare cases, an imperfection in the original, such as a blemish or missing page, may be replicated in our edition. We do, however, repair the vast majority of imperfections successfully; any imperfections that remain are intentionally left to preserve the state of such historical works.

Forgotten Books is a registered trademark of FB &c Ltd.
Copyright © 2015 FB &c Ltd.
FB &c Ltd, Dalton House, 60 Windsor Avenue, London, SW19 2RR.
Company number 08720141. Registered in England and Wales.

For support please visit www.forgottenbooks.com

1 MONTH OF FREE READING

at

www.ForgottenBooks.com

By purchasing this book you are eligible for one month membership to ForgottenBooks.com, giving you unlimited access to our entire collection of over 700,000 titles via our web site and mobile apps.

To claim your free month visit:

www.forgottenbooks.com/free553370

* Offer is valid for 45 days from date of purchase. Terms and conditions apply.

English
Français
Deutsche
Italiano
Español
Português

www.forgottenbooks.com

Mythology Photography **Fiction**
Fishing Christianity **Art** Cooking
Essays Buddhism Freemasonry
Medicine **Biology** Music **Ancient Egypt** Evolution Carpentry Physics
Dance Geology **Mathematics** Fitness
Shakespeare **Folklore** Yoga Marketing
Confidence Immortality Biographies
Poetry **Psychology** Witchcraft
Electronics Chemistry History **Law**
Accounting **Philosophy** Anthropology
Alchemy Drama Quantum Mechanics
Atheism Sexual Health **Ancient History**
Entrepreneurship Languages Sport
Paleontology Needlework Islam
Metaphysics Investment Archaeology
Parenting Statistics Criminology
Motivational

A HISTORY

OF

MARION COUNTY,

SOUTH CAROLINA,

From Its Earliest Times to the Present, 1901.

By W. W. SELLERS, Esq.,
of the Marion Bar.

COLUMBIA, S. C.
THE R. L. BRYAN COMPANY,
1902.

Allen County Public Library
900 Webster Street
PO Box 2270
Fort Wayne, IN 46801-2270

BETHEA.—The Bethea family will next be noticed. This very large and extensive family, both in name and in its vast network of connections, all sprang from one common stock, John Bethea, who emigrated from England to Virginia, at what precise time is not known, but supposed to be in the latter part of the seventeenth or early part of the eighteenth century. The name was originally spelled Berthier, and is supposed to be of French origin. The writer has been furnished, by Philip Y. Bethea, of Marion, with a family tree, and chart of the family from old "English John" up to date—at least, so far as Marion County is concerned, and I suppose generally, so far as can be ascertained. This chart only gives the names of males, no females—for the reason that they generally lost their identity by marriage; yet the females transmit the blood just as much as the males do—hence the writer will hereinafter notice the females as well as the males, in every instance where they are known. Old "English John" had two sons, John and Tristram. John settled in Nansemond County, Virginia, and Tristram settled on Cape Fear River, in North Carolina, as is supposed, in the early part of the eighteenth century. John, the second, had two sons, John, third, and William. John, third, emigrated to South Carolina, about the middle of the eighteenth century, or a little later, and settled on Buck Swamp, about two miles above the present town of Latta. His brother, William, about the same time, came to South Carolina (or they may have come together), and settled on Sweat Swamp, three or four miles above Harlleesville. These were the progenitors of all the Betheas and their numerous connections in Marion County, and, I suppose, throughout the Western States. Hereinafter these two families will be referred to as the "Buck Swamp family or set," and the "Sweat Swamp family or set." The wife of "Buck Swamp John" was Absala Parker, hence their youngest son was named "Parker." "Buck Swamp John" settled on the plantation now owned by one of his descendants, John C. Bethea, of Dillon; he was a prosperous man—took up and owned at the time of his death, in 1821, six or eight thousand acres of land around him and in near by parts, the most of which is now owned by some one or another of his descendants; he farmed and raised stock, drove it to Charleston; had and raised large orchards, raised fruit; made cider and brandy, and sold it, in his day, without let or hindrance; he accumulated a large estate for his day and time, which he gave almost entirely to his five sons, William, James, Philip, Elisha and Parker—giving nothing, comparatively, to his four daughters, Sallie, Pattie, Mollie and Absala (I think, was the name of the latter). Sallie married Levi Odom, of Revolutionary fame; two of them, Absala and Mollie, married a Mr. Owens; and Pattie married another Mr. Owens. None of them except Pattie have descendants in this State—as Sallie and Absala died childless, and Mollie and her Mr. Owens emigrated to Natchez, Miss. The five sons all settled, lived and died in Marion County. William, the eldest, married, first, a Miss Crawford; had one child, a son, John C. Bethea; his second wife was Mary (Polly) Sheckelford; the fruits of the marriage were five sons, Levi, Willam S., Frank, George J.

and Evander S. Bethea; the daughters were Rebecca, Absala, Mary, Catharine and Sarah Ann. Levi married Miss Mary Ann Bethea, a daughter of John Bethea, of the "Sweat Swamp set," and had two sons, Henry L. (who died in youth), and George, and four daughters, Sophia, Hannah Jane, Louisa and Charlotte. Of these, Sophia married William H. Smith, on Buck Swamp, and had and raised sons, Samuel O. Smith, Wm. B., Henry E. K. and John B. Smith, and two daughters, the wife of B. S. Ellis (first cousins), and Hamilton Edwards' wife. Hannah Jane Bethea married John C. Bass, and died childless. Louisa Bethea married James F. Galloway, and has a family of two sons, Henry and James, and four daughters, Sallie, Rebecca, Mary and Rachel. Charlotte Bethea married John E. Henry, who lives on the old William Bethea homestead, and has already been noticed in or among the Henry family. George Bethea, son of Levi, married a Miss Campbell, daughter of the late Edward Campbell, and has five sons, Edwin, Henry, Gary, Robert and Chalmers. Think Edwin lately married a Miss Smith, daughter of Marcus L. Smith. William S. Bethea, second son of William Bethea by his Sheckelford wife, married Miss Sarah Ann DeBerry, of Marlborough; by her he had two children, a daughter, Missouri, and a son, William Henry. Missouri became the first wife of John H. Hamer; she died, leaving one child, a son, Missouri Robert Hamer, who has already been noticed in or among the Hamer family. The son, William Henry Bethea, married, first, a Miss Wilson, of Wilmington, N. C., and by her he had two daughters, Adaline and Ella, both single, and two sons, Wilson and Henry (twins); Henry died in 1899; Wilson survives, and is unmarried. William Henry's first wife died, and he married, a second time, Miss Ellie Sherwood; she has one son, Evander S., a boy nearly grown. William Henry Bethea died in 1891 or 1892, *a felo de se.* Frank Bethea married, late in life, Miss Rebecca Manning, daughter of Woodward Manning; had one child, a son; father and son (an infant) both died the same year; the widow, Rebecca, married twice after that, and has already been mentioned among the Manning family. George J. Bethea married Miss Irena Page, daughter of Captain William Page; they had and raised two sons, William

A. and John D., and several daughters, Amanda, Ellen, Mary, Kittie and Belle. William A. married a Miss Floyd and moved to North Carolina. John D. married Miss Sallie Manning, daughter of Woodward Manning. Of the daughters, Amanda married William B. Ellen; Kittie married Joseph Watson, her first cousin; don't know who the others married. William A. has a son, named Jasper, and John D. has a son, named Herbert. Evander S. Bethea, the youngest son of old Buck Swamp William, never married. The oldest son of Buck Swamp William, by his Crawford wife, was named John C., born in 1798, and died January, 1863; married, first, a Widow Irby, whose maiden name was Allison; she had one child, a daughter, Elizabeth, when he married her, who grew up and married Henry Rogers, of Marlborough; they raised a large family of sons and daughters, and among the daughters is Henrietta, who is now the widow of the late Governor W. H. Ellerhe; by his marriage with the Widow Irby, he had and raised one son, Edwin Allison, when she died; and he afterwards married Sarah Ann Davis, and by her had and raised one son, John C., now of Dillon. Edwin A. married Ann Eliza Godbold, youngest daughter of Asa Godbold, Sr.; they live at Latta, and have a family of several sons and daughters; the sons are Asa, John C., Edwin and Reed Walker, and several daughters. One daughter married to W. C. McMillan, and is in Columbia, S. C. Asa has gone West; others all here. John C. Bethea, of Dillon, married Miss Hettie Bethea, daughter of W. W. Bethea, of Mississippi, and of the "Sweat Swamp family;" they have two sons. Horace and John C., and five daughters, all small. Of the sons of Buck Swamp William, there was one noticeable peculiarity—they all, except old John C., drank liquor excessively, and when intoxicated or drinking were perfectly quiet and harmless—much more so than when sober, except, perhaps, Evander S.; they were all capital men, energetic and progressive citizens. Of the daughters of old William Bethea (Buck Swamp), Rebecca married Colin McLellan, who has already been noticed in or among the McLellans. Absala married Hugh Campbell, already mentioned in or among the Campbells. Mary married William W. Bethea, of the "Sweat Swamp set," who will be noticed further on.

Catharine married Averitt N. Nance, of North Carolina, and raised one son, Daniel, and several daughters. Sarah Ann married a Mr. Folk, of North Carolina, and raised a family of two sons and two daughters, names unknown. All the sons and daughters of Buck Swamp William are dead; he himself died 13th June, 1840. James Bethea, the second son of old "Buck Swamp John," married Miss Margaret Cockrane, a daughter of Thomas Cockrane, of Marlborough County, and settled in the fork of Big and Little Reedy Creeks; they had and raised to be grown twelve children, five sons and seven daughters; the sons were Thomas C., Samuel J., John R., David and Claudius; the daughters were Nancy, Deborah, Sallie, Rachel, Lucinda, Lucretia and Jane. Thomas C. married Miss Miranza Rogers, a daughter of old Timothy Rogers, and emigrated to Mississippi. Samuel J. married Miss Mary Rogers, another daughter of old Timothy Rogers; he was local Methodist preacher for more than forty years, a man of high character and a most excellent citizen; he died in 1877; he married, a second time, Miss Elizabeth Bass, daughter of old man Joseph R. Bass; by his first marriage he had and raised to be grown eleven children—sons, James, Andrew J. and David N.; daughters, Sarah, Margaret, Harriet, Flora J., Louisa, Lucinda, Charlotte and Cattie; and by his last wife, one son, Samuel J., Jr. Of the sons, James died unmarried, just on arriving at manhood. Andrew J. was a practicing physician, and married Anna Maria Allen, daughter of Rev. Joel Allen, settled in the "Free State" section, and died in 1881, leaving his widow and five children—all now grown—three sons, Herbert, Percy and Andrew, and two daughters, Mrs. Rev. Pearce Kilgo, who has five children, and Mrs. William T. Bethea, who has three children, sons, James Earle, William Thaddeus, Jr., and Philip Osborne. The next son of Rev. S. J. Bethea, David N., who died last week, married, first, Anna J. Sellers, daughter of the writer, and settled in the "Free State" section; they had eight children, three of whom are dead, also the mother; of the eight, five were sons and three daughters; the sons were William T., Samuel Stoll, David A., Swinton Legare and Andrew Pearce; the daughters were Cattie May, Lillian and Anna Laval. Of these, Samuel Stoll,

David A. and Cattie May are dead—died before majority. William Thaddeus married his cousin, Georgia Bethea, as above stated and children as above stated; he is railroad agent at Dillon and has been for more than ten years, and Mayor of the town for three years. By the second marriage of Rev. S. J. Bethea, he had one son, Samuel J., Jr., who is and has been for ten years or more a traveling Methodist preacher in the South Carolina Conference; he married Miss Nannie Bethea, of the "Sweat Swamp" family, and have only one child, a son, Samuel J., Jr. Of the daughters of Rev. S. J. Bethea, three, Lucinda, Cattie and Charlotte, all grown young ladies, died unmarried. Sarah married James Moore, of Marlborough County; they had only one child, a son, James B. Moore, of Latta; the father died when James B. was an infant; the widow never married again, and died a few years ago. The son, James B. Moore, married Miss Mollie Godbold, daughter of Asa Godbold, Jr.; they have three children living, two sons, Clancy and LaCoste, and a daughter, Lorena (small). Margaret, the next daughter of Rev. S. J. Bethea, married John W. Tart; they had and raised three sons, James, John and Andrew; the father and mother are both dead. James went to Savannah, married a Miss Fuller, of Waycross, Ga., and when last heard of was said to be doing well. John married a Miss Bethea, daughter of Elisha Bethea, Jr., of Latta; they have some family, how many and of what sex is not known. Andrew Tart married a Miss Hays, daughter of Hamilton R. Hays, and lives near Kirby's Cross Roads; suppose they have some family, how many and of what sex is unknown. Of the daughters of John W. Tart and wife, two or three of them died unmarried, after maturity. One married Samuel O. Smith, of Buck Swamp; they have a large family. Their oldest, a son, Stephen Lane Smith, lives at Latta, and lately married a Miss Edwards, a daughter of Austin Edwards. Another daughter married C. C. Gaillard, and has three children—a daughter, Maggie, and a son, Luther, and another name unknown; they now live at Dillon; their children are grown. Another daughter married James Johnson, a nephew of Chancellor W. D. Johnson, called "Black Jim," to distinguish him from J. W. Johnson, Esq., another nephew and son-in-law of the Chancellor; they live at Fair Bluff, N. C.; they have some children, how many and of what sex is unknown. Another and youngest daughter of John W. Tart and his wife, Margaret, married Solon Lewis, of Latta; she died some months ago, and left two children, a daughter and a son, I think. The next daughter of Rev. S. J. Bethea, Harriet, and the only survivor of his eleven first children, has never married, and is sixty-one or two years old. Flora, the next daughter, married the late Stephen D. Lane; both are dead, and died childless. Louisa, the next daughter, married Newton Owens, of North Carolina; they moved to Texas several years ago; she is dead, leaving several children, sons and daughters—perhaps, all grown. John R. Bethea, the third son of old James Bethea, married Miss Harriet Bass, daughter of old Joseph R. Bass. I think this family has been already noticed in or among the Bass family. The fourth son of old James Bethea, David, died a young man, unmarried, in 1843. Claudius Bethea, the fifth and youngest son of old James Bethea, married, late in life, Miss Mary Ann Miles, daughter of Charles Miles, of the "Free State" section; he and his wife are both dead, childless. Of the daughters of old James Bethea, the eldest, Nancy, married Salathel Moody, an older brother of old Barfield Moody; they had several children, sons and daughters, some grown, when they broke up and moved West. Deborah, the second daughter, married James Spears, a very successful man in Marlborough; they had and raised a large family—two sons, Andrew J. and Edwin A., and six or seven daughters; they have descendants, grand-sons, in Marion County now, in the persons of Dr. J. H. David and Frank B. David,* enterprising, progressive men, with their families. They have many descendants in Marlborough County. The two sons, Andrew J. and Edwin A., died childless; Edwin married. Lucinda, the fifth daughter of old James Bethea, married Colonel Wilie Bridges, of Marlborough, and emigrated West. Sallie, the third daughter, married Willis Crawford, from whom sprang several sons and two daughters; the sons were James, Hardy, Thomas C., Willis, William and Gibson G. Crawford, now of Latta; the daughters were Rhoda and Margaret. Of the sons, James died when about grown,

---

*Frank B. David died recently.

unmarried. Hardy married a Miss Platt, and went West. Thomas C. married twice, is well known in the county; married, the last time, a Miss McPherson, in West Marion, and has resided there for more than thirty years; his wife died a short time ago, childless; he is a most excellent man and a good citizen.* Willis Crawford was a physician; married a lady in Charleston, and was soon after accidentally killed in a fox drive by his own gun—verifying the adage, "That more people are killed or hurt at play than at work." William died, a single man, after having gone through the war and came out unhurt. G. G. Crawford married Miss Kate Bethea, daughter of Colonel James R. Bethea; they had and raised two sons, James C. and Samuel B., and two daughters, Jessie and Mary; his wife is dead; he has not remarried. James G. has lately married a Miss Evans, of Society Hill. Jessie married, two or three years ago, William Ellis Bethea; no offspring. Samuel B. and Mary are yet single. The oldest daughter of Willis and Sallie Crawford, Rhoda, married Henry Easterling, and has already been noticed among the Easterlings. Margaret, the youngest daughter, never married, and is dead. Rachel, the fourth daughter of old James Bethea, married Enoch Meekins, of Marlborough; he, however, settled and lived many years near Harlleesville, and raised a considerable family of sons and daughters, and finally moved to North Carolina, where he and his wife both died; don't know enough about his children to trace them. He had one son, Philip B., who married a Miss Hays, daughter of John C. Hays; they also moved to North Carolina, and are lost sight of. One daughter married John R. Carmichael; he died, and left two sons, Alexander and McCoy, and one daughter, Johny; the mother still lives. Another daughter married James McGirt; they went to North Carolina. Lucretia, the sixth daughter, first married Aaron Meekins, of Marlborough, brother of Enoch, who had married Rachel; Aaron Meekins lived but a short time, and died childless; the widow afterwards married Wesley Stackhouse, who has already been noticed among the Stackhouse family. Jane, the youngest daughter, married Tristram Easterling, who has already been noticed in or among the Easterling family. Philip Be-

---

*Thomas C. Crawford has recently died.

thea, the third son of old "Buck Swamp John," married, in 1801, Rachel Cochrane, daughter of old Thomas Cochrane, of Marlborough, and sister of his brother James' wife. (As to Thomas Cochrane—he was a Vermonter, ran away from his parents in Vermont when a mere lad, and married a Miss Council, and settled on Great Pee Dee, just above the mouth of Crooked Creek; raised a family; married three times; the two Bethea's wives above mentioned were daughters of the first wife, together with another daughter, Polly, who became the wife of old John Hamer, and the progenitress of the large family of that name in Marlborough and Marion, and a son, named Robert; he amassed a large property and lived to a great age.) Philip Bethea settled on Catfish, where he lived and died in 1865; they raised to be grown two sons, Elisha C. and James R., and three daughters, Clarissa, Margaret and Martha Ann. Of the sons, Elisha C. married Martha Ann Walters, daughter of Jeremiah Walters, of upper Marion; Captain Elisha C. was a very successful man as a farmer and well to do in life; they had eleven sons and four daughters; the sons were Philip W., John J., Robert C., James A., Elisha, Picket, Morgan, George, William W., Clarence and Julius N.; the daughters were Elizabeth Ann, Wilmina R., Augusta B. and Alice. Of the sons of Elisha C., Philip W. married Miss Anna Smith, a daughter of Rev. John L. Smith, of the "Fork" section, and settled where he now lives; his family has been noted among the Lane family. The second son of Captain Elisha C. Bethea is Dr. John J. Bethea, at Mullins; has been practicing medicine since 1852; he married, first, Miss Mary Bethea, a daughter of Tristram Bethea, of Floral College, one of the "Cape Fear set;" she had one child, a daughter, Emma, who grew up and married Dr. William Harrel, who moved to Georgia some years ago, and had when they left six daughters and no son. Dr. John J. Bethea married, a second time, Miss Jane Smith, a daughter of Rev. John L. Smith, and sister of his Brother Philip's wife. Owing to some trouble growing out of the war, Dr. John had to leave the county and State for fear of the Federal garrison stationed at Marion in 1865 to 1868; he went to Mississippi, and his family soon followed after him, and he stayed in that State some fifteen or twenty years, when he came back, and has been in this county ever since. His family have been noticed in tracing the Lane family. Robert C. Bethea, the third son of Captain Elisha C., married, some time before the war, a Miss Legette, daughter of John C. Legette, of West Marion; before the war, he removed to Mississippi; they had some little family before leaving this county—know nothing more of them; he was also a physician, and in his adopted home he became a local Methodist preacher. James A. Bethea, the fourth son of Captain Elisha C., was a bright young man; volunteered in the early part of the war, was a Lieutenant or rose to a Lieutenancy in Co. E, Twenty-third Regiment, S. C. V., and remained in the war to the end, a gallant soldier. After the war he went to Mississippi; and from there went to a law school at Lebanon, Tenn.; returned to Mississippi, was admitted to the bar, but soon after took sick and died—a worthy and promising young man; he never married. Elisha Bethea, Jr., the fifth son of Captain Elisha C., married, on the 9th March, 1861—the writer officiating at the nuptials—to Miss Sallie Ellis, daughter of the Widow Ginsy Ellis. He also volunteered and went into the army, and remained in it till he was disabled for field service, when he came home, and for some time his friends supposed he would not survive the wounds, but he did and has been going on crutches ever since—the wound being in his hip; he yet lives, and is near Latta, an energetic and successful man, a farmer. He had by his first wife several sons and daughters. His oldest living son, William Ellis, is now merchandising at Latta, and has been twice married—first, a Georgia lady, who had three sons, Charles, Robert and Dallas, and one daughter, Florence, and died; he married, a second time, Miss Jessie Crawford; she has no children. Arthur, his second son, has lately married a Miss Hays, of Hillsboro Township, a daughter of William B. Hays; he teaches school. Morgan, his third son, is a young man, unmarried; he teaches school. Of his daughters by his first marriage, one, Mattie, married John J. George, who died childless. Another, Carrie, married John Tart; they have five children (small). Another, Augusta, is unmarried. Another, Nellie, married Tristram Hamilton; she has two children, Bertha and Sallie (small). Elisha Bethea, Jr., had another son, Benjamin, and one named Elisha; both died in youth. Elisha Bethea's first wife, Sallie, died; he married again, her sister, Mary Ann, who at the time of her marriage was the Widow Thomas; by this second marriage he has one son, named Power, who is now in Wofford College, and a daughter, named Eva, and perhaps others (small). Pickett Bethea, the sixth son of Captain Elisha C., married Miss Carrie Honour, daughter of Rev. John H. Honour, of Charleston, about the first of the war; by this marriage two sons were born, Walker and Pickett. Walker died when a child. Pickett K. grew up and became a doctor, and married a Miss Davis, of North Carolina, and has removed to Socastee, in Horry County, and is there practicing medicine, and is said to be doing well. His father, Pickett, volunteered early in the war, and was a Lieutenant in Captain McKerall's company, in 25th Regiment; he was killed in one of the battles in Virginia, in 1863. His widow married again to J. W. Saintclair, a school teacher; they removed West; she had several children for him, and died. Morgan, the seventh son of Captain Elisha C., volunteered early in the war; he sickened and died at home while on a furlough; he was unmarried. George, the eighth son, was killed, when about thirteen or fourteen years of age, by what was called a "flying mare"—another verification of the adage "that more people are killed or hurt at play than at work." William W. Bethea, the ninth son of Captain Elisha C., now living in West Marion, married Miss Sallie Morrison, a daughter of Rev. Mr. Morrison, a Presbyterian minister, of Anson County, N. C., a very estimable and accomplished lady; the fruits of this marriage are four sons, Morrison, Theodore, Oscar and James. Of these, Morrison is married to a lady of Clinton (name unknown), and has two sons, Curtis and Eugene; there may be a daughter or two (all small). William W. Bethea may have daughters, the writer does not know. One of the sons, Theodore (I believe) is a graduate of the Citadel Academy of Charleston—said to have graduated with distinction. Clarence, the tenth son of Captain Elisha C., died when a small boy. Julius N., the eleventh son of Captain Elisha C., married, first, Miss Anna Shrewsberry, daughter of the late Edward C. Shrewsberry, of the "Free State" section. An incident of their marriage may be here related: They were married at a school house near by her father's, in the woods on a road not much frequented, by the Rev. Joel Allen, on Christmas day, in 1871; he gave them a certificate of their marriage Only one person was present at the nuptials besides themselves and the officiating clergyman; and at their special instance and request, the marriage was to be kept secret until the 19th day of April following, it being Julius' birth-day and the day of his arrival at the age of twenty-one years. Julius carried his wife back to her home, half a mile away, and left her there; he went to his father's, and said nothing until the appointed time, 19th April, 1872, when he told his father and mother about it, and went to her father's, and their marriage was satisfactorily established to her parents, and he took her and carried her to his father's. A sufficient reason, satisfactory to them, may have existed for their marriage and subsequent secrecy, but it does not accord with the writer's views of propriety, nor with the conduct of 999 out of 1,000. His bride was a very intellectual and well cultivated lady—far more so than many in that region; the fruits of the marriage were three sons, Herbert, Ernest and Adger, and one or two daughters, one named Mattie May—suppose they are all grown. Anna, his first wife, died, and he married, a second time, Miss Carrie Sessions, daughter of John D. Sessions, of Marion; they reside now at Mullins; children of the last marriage, if any, are small—names, number and sex unknown. Of the daughters of Captain Elisha C. Bethea, the eldest, Elizabeth Ann, married John B. Bethea, of the "Sweat Swamp" family; her mother was a half Bethea of the same set; he had previously gone to Mississippi, and came back to her home in Marion County and married; the bridal trip was to be to Mississippi. She had some negroes, which her father had given her, and they with their little baggage were taken along for the trip. This was before the war, about 1856. When the bridal party arrived at Marion to take the train, the groom put the bride on board, and stepped back to see to getting on the negroes—a woman and some children, and whilst thus engaged the train pulled off and left him; of course, he ran after it and tried to stop it, but failed in his almost frantic efforts. His bride went on to Florence (then a small village) and stopped over for the night; the groom spent the night in Marion and went over the next day and joined his wife. I will leave the reader to imagine whether there was intense disappointment or not, and whether there was any cursing done by the groom. The bridal party went to Mississippi and settled there—I think, in Smith County. John B. was a very energetic and persevering man, a farmer; he went into the war, and in 1863, he died of disease, and left his wife and four sons, Augustus B., William, Sumter and John—the latter born after his father's death, all then small. After John B.'s death, Captain Elisha C. went out to Mississippi and brought the widow and her children to this county. The widow settled on a place given her by her father, and went to work to raise and educate her sons; in this she succeeded well. She was no ordinary woman; well educated herself and of fine literary taste, and to this added her fine business qualifications and her success, placed her in the front rank among women. Much more might be said to her credit, but space will not permit a further extended notice. Her sons grew up and one by one they went to Birmingham, Ala., and she finally followed and, I think, yet lives. The second daughter of Captain Elisha C., Wilmina Rachel, has never married, and is now in the sixtieth year of her age. The third daughter, Augusta B., married A. E. Gilchrist, of Mullins, and has already been noticed herein among the Gilchrist family. Alice, the fourth and youngest daughter of Captain Elisha C., married D. Asbury Smith, who has already been noticed among the Lane family. She, too, has gone to Birmingham, Ala., where three of her four sons reside.

According to the chart of the Bethea family in all its branches, including the Nansemond County, Va., Betheas, the Cape Fear, N. C., Betheas, the "Buck Swamp set," and the "Sweat Swamp set," Captain Elisha C. Bethea "takes the cake" for having and raising the greatest number of sons, eleven; while Dr. J. F. Bethea stands next, with eight. Not much danger of extinction. Colonel James R. Bethea, the second and youngest son of old man Philip Bethea, who has been mentioned in several places herein before in connection with other matters, married, rather late in life (thirty-four or thirty-five years old), to Miss Mary McLeod, of Marlborough, one of the best and most devotedly pious women I ever met; and should any of her children turn out badly in the future, it cannot be charged to any fault in the mother's training, either by precept or example; they had and raised (Jessie, the oldest, was near grown when he died) six sons and three daughters; the sons were Jessie, James D., Philip Y., Elisha, D. McLeod and Robert Lucien; the daughters were Kate, Clara and M. Isabella. Of the sons, Jessie died when about grown. James D., the second son, married Miss Flora Fore, daughter of the late Stephen Fore; she is dead. Of James D.'s family, mention has already been made in or among the Fore family. Philip Y., the third son, now in Marion, a first class business man; has been County Auditor, and is now and has been for ten or more years cashier of the Bank of Marion; married Miss Florence Johnson, of Charleston, a distant relative of his—his father and Florence's grand-mother, Sallie Strobel, were first cousins; they have had six sons (one, Philip Y., dead), Eugene, Arthur, Johnson, Stewart, Philip Y. and Markley, and three daughters, Eloise, Edith and Mary McLeod—none of whom are married. Eugene, the eldest, is in the Philippines or China, in the United States army, an officer, a promising young man, and may rise to greater distinction. The other children are all at home—Eloise and Arthur are grown. Philip Y. has a very interesting family; his wife is a superior woman, and well fitted by education and early training to raise a family. Elisha, the fourth son of Colonel J. R. Bethea, was quite a promising young man, but the fates decreed that he should not live, and he died when twenty-five or six years of age, unmarried. D. McLeod Bethea, the fifth son of Colonel J. R. Bethea, a first class man, an excellent and successful farmer, married Miss Florence Fore, daughter of the late Stephen Fore, and who, with his family, have already been mentioned herein in or among the Fore family. Robert Lucien, the sixth son of Colonel Bethea, has married twice; first, a Miss Shaw, of Bishopville; by her he had one child, a daughter, Leona, who is now nearly grown. The first wife died, and he married, a second time, to Miss Rosa Carnes, of Bishopville, and by her has some three or four children; names and sex unknown; they are yet children. Robert Lucien lives in Bishopville, and runs a hotel.* Of the daughters of Colonel J. R. Bethea, the eldest, Kate, married Gibson G. Crawford; both of whom and their family have already been noticed herein among the Betheas above. The second daughter of Colonel Bethea, Clara, married Holland Manning, who lives on her patrimony, and are doing well—in fact, Clara is an extra smart and sensible woman; they have two children, daughters, both children, Mary Belle and Hope. Holland Manning was a widower with five children, three of whom are married; he has a place of his own in extreme upper Marion, which he rents. Colonel James R. Bethea died in 1878, at sixty-nine years of age, and his widow, Mary, some years afterward. The youngest daughter, Isabella, or Belle, has never married; she has a good farm, which she rents; she also teaches school, and when not thus engaged she stays with her sister, Clara Manning.

Colonel James R. Bethea, when young, imbibed a military spirit, and manifested a strong ambition to attain to high honors in the militia of the State. Starting as a private in his local beat company (Cross Roads), he soon obtained a Lieutenancy; and from that to the Captaincy of the company; and from that to Major of the upper battalion; and by seniority soon became Lieutenant Colonel of the regiment; and from that by election to the Colonelcy of the Thirty-second Regiment, which position he held at the time of his marriage, in March, 1844, and continued to hold that position for three or four years afterward—and in the meantime declined to be a candidate for Brigadier General, to which place he could have been elected, perhaps, without opposition. He was an efficient officer, and was popular as such. It was very expensive, and as he had a growing family he wisely chose to abandon the further pursuit of military honors (empty as they were), and devote his means to the support and education of his fast-growing family. He resigned his commission as Colonel, and Elly Godbold or John J. George was elected in his place. They both were successive Colonels, but do not remember which of the two were first elected. Afterwards Colonel Bethea was elected as a Representative from the district in the State Legislature (1848 to 1850).

---

*He is now at Dillon in the same business.

Of the daughters of Philip Bethea, a son of old "Buck Swamp John," Clarissa, the eldest, never married, and died in 1861, at the age of fifty-eight. The second daughter, Margaret, married Willis Finklea, called Arter Willis; in a short while Finklea moved to Alabama; there they had several children, five of whom were raised. Willis Finklea was a drinking man and treated his wife badly, so much so that she could not stand it; they separated, and her father, in 1841, went to Alabama, Monroe County, in a wagon, and brought her and her five children back to Marion County; Finklea soon after died; her children were raised mainly by her father; there were two sons, James C. and William; the daughters were Lucinda, Sallie and Margaret Agnes. James C. Finklea is now one of our fellow-citizens, known as Captain Finklea, in Wahee Township, and, in fact, all over the county. Captain Finklea volunteered in Captain C. J. Fladger's Company E, 23d South Carolina Regiment, in the Confederate War; went off as a Sergeant in that company. Captain Fladger in a few months resigned, and Harris Covington, First Lieutenant, became Captain, the other Lieutenants went up, and Captain Finklea was elected Third Lieutenant, made vacant. Some time after Covington resigned, and the company was reorganized by orders from the proper authorities, and Captain Finklea was elected Captain of the company, and served gallantly until the latter part of 1864 —having fought through all the campaigns from Virginia to Mississippi. At that time Captain Finklea was the senior Captain in the regiment, when by the casualties of war the Major's office became vacant, and according to rules of promotion, Captain Finklea was entitled to the place; but a Junior Captain was promoted, by appointment, not by election, to the Majoralty over him; when Captain Finklea resigned and came home, and did not return to the service. It was said he was a good and brave Captain; that his men all loved and respected him, but he was not popular with the higher officers, because he always associated with his men and not with them. Captain Finklea is known as a modest, retiring man; not self-asserting. Had the vacancy for Major been left to his company, he would have gotten the vote of every man; he sympathized with his men, fared as they fared, and assumed no superiority over them on account of his position. As an evidence of Captain Finklea's popularity, when he was first elected County Commissioner, a few years ago (he was twice elected), he received every vote at Berry's Cross Roads, something over 200. He is a man of good sense, a good and safe manager of his farm and home affairs, unostentatious and unassuming, rather avoids company— unfortunately, of late years, his habits are not good. After the war he went, first, to Alabama and then to Texas, where he married a Miss Kyle; she had one child for him, a son, who died in infancy, and the mother died; he then came back to South Carolina, and married the widow of Dr. William H. Godbold, a most excellent and cultured woman; by her he had one son, named for his first wife, a very promising boy, but he died at the age of four or five years. William Finklea, the youngest brother, died when about grown. Lucinda, the oldest daughter, married John T. Kinney, of Marlborough, and emigrated to Texas, where they raised a family; both are dead, and nothing is known further of them. Sallie, the second daughter, married Cyrus B. Haselden; they had and raised five children, two sons, John and Frank, and three daughters, Lucy, Maggie and Fannie. Cyrus B. Haselden and wife, Sallie, and family, have already been noticed in or among the Haseldens. Margaret Agnes, the youngest daughter of Willis Finklea and wife, Margaret, never married, and died of cancer on the breast, at the age of forty, in March, 1882. A noble girl she was. Martha Ann Bethea, the third and youngest daughter of old man Philip Bethea, married W. W. Sellers, the writer, 10th January, 1847, and died 2d February, 1893; they had seven children, four sons, John C., William W., Benjamin Morgan and Philip B.; of these, Benjamin Morgan died a little under two years of age; three daughters, Anna Jane, Rachel C. and Mary O. Of the sons, John C. is a graduate of the South Carolina College, studied law, was admitted to the bar in 1870, was elected to the Legislature in 1870, practiced law only one year, and retired on the farm where he now lives; his first wife was Miss Maggie E. Mace, daughter of the late John Mace; she had seven children, three sons, Benjamin B., John M. and Wallace Duncan; of these, John M. died under one year old; there were four daughters, Lucy B., Annie R., Maggie Leila and Maggie Ellen (called Pearl). Benjamin B. Sellers is a graduate of Wofford College; married Miss Norma Watson, voungest daughter of the late William Watson; they have two children, Harry and Margaret Ellen; he is farming. Wallace Duncan's education is not completed. Of the daughters, Lucy B. is a graduate of the Columbia Female College; she married D. Maxcy Watson; they have no children. Annie R. went to the Female College for more than a year, but did not graduate; is unmarried. Maggie Leila is near grown, is going to school. Maggie E., called Pearl, was only three days old when her mother died; her Aunt Rachel Norton took her and has so far raised her; she is near thirteen years of age. W. W. Sellers, Jr., married Miss Harriet J. McPherson, daughter of C. Ervin McPherson, of West Marion; they have had seven or eight children, only three of whom are living—two daughters, Rachel Elise and Etta; the son is Marvin McSwain—none of them grown. W. W. Sellers, Jr., is one of the Chiefs in the present State Constabulary, and has been for several years; he resides at Latta. Philip B. Sellers is a graduate of Wofford College; studied law and was admitted to the bar in 1884 (May); he married Miss M. Sue DuBois, daughter of J. T. DuBois, of Marion, in December, 1886; they have five children, three sons, John DuBois, Philip Bruce and William Maynard, and two daughters, Agnes Leona and Mildred Eugenia—all children, none grown; he resides at Dillon, and is actively engaged in the practice of his chosen profession, with apparent success. Of the daughters of the writer and his wife, Anna Jane, the eldest daughter married her cousin, D. N. Bethea; he and Anna Jane and their family have been already noticed in the same connection, Betheas. The second daughter of W. W. Sellers and wife married Hon. James Norton, of Mullins; they had but two children, sons, Evan Lewis and William Fitzroy. Evan Lewis, the eldest, died when four or five years of age. William Fitzroy grew up to manhood; first went to Wofford College, and after two years spent there, he went to the law department of the South Carolina College for two years, graduated in law, and *ipso facto* became a lawyer—he does not practice, however; he married Miss Florence Smith, daughter of B. Gause Smith, at Mullins; they reside at Mullins, and have no children. Mary O. Sellers, youngest daughter of W. W. Sellers, married Thomas N. Godbold, a son of Dr. W. H. Godbold; they have only three children living, Thomas Carroll, Anna and Bessie. Thomas N. Godbold is in the railroad service, on the "Plant System" between Charleston and Savannah. This family has already been noticed in or among the Goldbold family. Recurring back a few lines: John C. Sellers, after living about ten years a widower, married, a second time, to Miss Jaquiline Oliver, of North Carolina, 2d February, 1898—a most excellent woman; they have had two children, boys, who are both dead. Elisha Bethea, fourth son of old "Buck Swamp John," known as old Colonel Elisha, never married. It is said of him that he was a very handsome man in his young days; he was born in 1787, and was Captain of a company in the war of 1812-14; he was better educated than any of his brothers—in fact, better than most men of his day. His father left him a fine property, his homestead and a large number of negroes; few men of that time had such a prospect. He was very popular and had more natural politeness than any Bethea I ever saw. But, alas! the demon of intemperance ruined him; he died poor in 1854, at the age of sixty-seven years. After the war of 1812, he became Colonel of the militia. He was true to his friends and true to his country. It seemed to be his delight to make others pleasant, happy and comfortable even at the expense of his own convenience. This was the man after he became poor, which proved it to be natural with him. His bearing and appearance in poverty and old age was that of a nobleman, of a cavalier. Parker Bethea, the youngest son of old "Buck Swamp John," was born in 1790, and was given his mother's maiden name, Parker; he settled opposite the head of Catfish, at the Cross Roads on the Marlborough line, twenty-two miles above Marion, and died there, St. John the Evangelist Day, 27th December, 1867; he married Elizabeth Harllee, daughter of old Thomas Harllee; they raised two sons, Harllee and Benjamin Parker, and four or five daughters. Harllee had one son, Reddin, and Benj. P. had one named Charles. Harllee moved to Florida many years ago; his wife was a Miss Roberts—Benj. P.'s wife was a Miss Woolvin; he moved just after the war to Pender or Onslow County, N. C., thirty miles on the coast above Wilmington. These families have already been noticed in or among the Roberts family and the Harllee family.

One more remark about these old Betheas, sons of "Buck Swamp John." They all loved liquor and, except old Philip, drank it to excess, till after middle life, when they tapered off, and by the time of old age became perfectly abstemious, and this was specially the case with William, James and Parker. They were all good men and excellent citizens, and did much in starting the development of the resources of the county. The first gin house built in the county was built by old "Buck Swamp John;" it stood on what has ever since been called the "Gin House Branch," near the Cross Roads, at John C. Bethea's plantation; a good part of that gin house is still in use. After the death of old "Buck Swamp John," in 1821, the plantation fell to old Colonel Elisha, and he in his financial extremities years afterwards sold the gin house to Cross Roads Henry Berry; he pulled it down and hauled it to Berry's Cross Roads, and it stands there now, the property of James Berry, between his (James Berry's) dwelling and the storehouse. It has been there, to the writer's knowledge, more than sixty years.

Of the grand-sons of old "English John," John settled on Buck Swamp, as already stated, and William settled on Sweat Swamp; he married, and had four sons, John, Goodman, Philip and Jessie. Of these, John, the man who, after the Revolution, hung the Tory, Snowden, married, and he had and raised four sons, William, Tristram, John and Cade—the latter, no doubt, is remembered by many now living in upper Marion and elsewhere in the county. Goodman Bethea married and had two sons, Philip and Jessie. Philip, the brother of Goodman, never married, or if he did, he had no children. Jessie, the fourth son of old "Sweat Swamp William," had Hugh Goodman, William, Henry and Tristram. According to the Bethea chart none of these latter five had any posterity. Supposed they emigrated to parts unknown or died in youth. William, the grand-son of "Sweat Swamp William," had seven sons, John, Tristram, Philip, Jessie, William, Thomas C. and Cade. Of these latter, John, William, Thomas C. and Cade had no offspring. Cade is in upper Marion now an old man.* Of the other three, Tristram had one son, named William; Philip had four sons, Jessie, William, Tristram and Philip—these last four seem to have had no offspring. Jessie, the great-grand-son of old "Sweat Swamp William," had five sons, John, William, Charles, Farquehard and Holden; their mother was a Miss Bethune; she had some daughters, one the wife (now dead) of Patrick Finagan. By the Bethea chart now lying before me, none of these five latter Betheas have any offspring, but the writer knows to the contrary. John has twelve or thirteen children, boys and girls. Holden married Miss Alice Rogers, daughter of Jessie Rogers, and has some children. The Bethune wife of Jessie Bethea had a daughter other than Mrs. Finagan, who was the wife of the late Edward C. Shrewsberry. Tristram, the grand-son of old "Sweat Swamp William," married and had one son, Philip, who was a lawyer, but did not practice much here, and soon went to Alabama, and his father soon after moved himself there; father and son have been lost sight of—suppose both are long since dead. John, another grand-son of "Sweat Swamp William," married Miss Hannah Walker; by the marriage four sons, William W., Alfred W., David W. and John B., were had and raised, and five daughters, Sophia, Mary Ann, Charlotte, Sallie and Hannah. Of the sons, William W. married, first, Mary Bethea, a granddaughter of "Buck Swamp John;" they had three sons, John F., Dallas and William; don't know of any daughters by William W.'s first marriage; he married, a second time, Miss Mary Platt, a daughter of old Daniel Platt; by his (Platt's) second marriage with Polly Lane, a daughter of old James C. Lane, who was a son of old Osborne Lane, I know of but two children; by William W. Bethea's second marriage, two daughters—Hettie, the wife of John C. Bethea, of Dillon, who has already been mentioned; the other daughter married a Mr. Floyd, a son of Judge Floyd, of Alabama or Mississippi. J. F. Bethea (our Dr. Frank Bethea) married his first cousin, Hannah Jane, daughter and only child of Dr. Alfred W. Bethea; by this marriage eight sons, Alfred, Preston L., Tristram, William, Frank, Charles, Archie and Victor, and, I think, three

---
*Died recently.

daughters, Flora and two others whose names are not known, have been born. Alfred (I think) died about the time of his majority. Preston L. married a Miss Weatherby, daughter of Colon W. Weatherby, of Bennettsville, and resides at Dillon. Tristram married a Miss McRae, daughter of Hon. James McRae, of Albriton, in extreme upper Marion; he resides at Dillon. Frank married a Miss Smith, of Alabama or Georgia, and is now a resident of one of those States. William recently married a Miss McLeod, of Robeson County, N. C. The other three sons are yet with their father, Dr. Frank, I suppose, not grown. Of the daughters of Dr. J. F. Bethea, the eldest, Flora, married Tristram Thompson; she was a most excellent lady, loved and respected by all who knew her. The Doctor's two other daughters are minors and still with him. Dr. J. F. Bethea is a successful man every way; as a farmer, he is a man of affairs, a turpentine and saw mill man, is merchandizing at Dillon, he and his sons (don't know how many or which), under the firm name of J. F. Bethea & Co.; he has once represented the county in the State Legislature. Dallas Bethea, brother of Dr. J. F. Bethea, is in Mississippi; he has three sons, William, Preston and Franklin. Alfred W., another great-grand-son of "Sweat Swamp William," married Flora Bethea, a daughter of Tristram Bethea, of Floral College, who was one of the "Cape Fear set," and by her had only one child, a daughter, Hannah Jane, who married Dr. J. F. Bethea, with the results above stated. Dr. Alfred W. Bethea was no ordinary man; he was eminent as a physician, a good farmer, a well-informed man and of sound practical sense and judgment; he was a member of the Secession Convention of 1860; he was waylaid, shot and killed by the deserters in the last months of the war, much regretted by all who knew him; he lived where Dr. J. F. Bethea now lives; the widow, who survived him, is now dead. David W. Bethea, another great-grand-son of "Sweat Swamp William," married, first, Miss Sarah Jane Manning, daughter of Mealy Manning, of Marlborough; by her he had two sons, LeRoy and David W., they are both married. LeRoy has two sons, Henry and Leon—these have already been mentioned in or among the Mannings and Easterlings, to which reference is made. David W., Jr., has lately married, I think, a Miss

Townsend, of North Carolina; gives promise of becoming a useful man—is already so; if like his mother he cannot be otherwise, as she was one of the best of women. D. W. Bethea, Sr., represented the county one time in the Legislature, 1860-1862; he was a good citizen; he married, a second time, a Miss Brunson, of Darlington, who yet survives; no offspring. John B. Bethea (the youngest), another great-grand-son of "Sweat Swamp William," married Elizabeth A. Bethea, a daughter of Captain Elisha C., of the "Buck Swamp set;" they had four sons, as already mentioned among the "Buck Swamp set," to which reference is made. Of the daughters of John Bethea, the grand-son of "Sweat Swamp William," as given herein above, Sophia, the eldest, married Robert B. Platt, and in a few weeks or months after her marriage she was accidentally burned to death, and, of course, died childless. Mary Ann, the second daughter, married Levi Bethea, of the "Buck Swamp set," and has already been herein noticed in the "Buck Swamp set," to which reference is made. Charlotte and Sallie, the third and fourth daughters, both married the same evening—Charlotte to Zack Fulmore and Sallie to Dr. John K. Alford, both of North Carolina, where they thereafter lived and died; know but little of the family of either. Hannah, the fifth and youngest daughter, married Alexander Fulmore, of North Carolina; they moved to Alabama; know nothing of them. Cade Bethea, the youngest grand-son of old "William of Sweat Swamp," through his son, John, married Kittie Bethea, a sister of "Floral College Tristram," and a great-granddaughter of Tristram, the son of "English John," who settled on Cape Fear River, N. C.—her father being Jessee and her grand-father was Jessee, whose father was Tristram, the settler on Cape Fear, whose father was old "English John." This I get from the chart now lying before me. Cade Bethea and Kittie had and raised five sons and three daughters; the sons were John W., Evander R., William C., Calvin and Henry; the daughters were Caroline, Harriet and Mary Ann. Cade Bethea settled on Sweat Swamp, north side, just opposite the mouth of Beaver Dam, on the south side, where he lived and died; I think the place now belongs to Hon. D. W. McLaurin. There was but one Cade Bethea in regard to character; he was an incessant talker, and in his latter days was always on the go, around among his kinsfolk and friends; was a great complainer and murmurer, and to hear him tell it, he was going to come to nothing—going to perish to death. An illustration of his character in this regard may be here related: On one occasion, his nephew, Creek Jessie Bethea, went to see his Uncle Cade, in the month of July or August; the old gentleman was in his piazza —it was a very hot day; the old man was complaining and murmuring as usual, that his crop was a complete failure, that he was not going to make anything, and he and his family would all perish in a pile. After a while, Jessie, his nephew, proposed that they would go out and look around his crop; the old man did not want to go; said he did not want to see it—it made him sick to look at it; they, however, went, and after looking around and seeing it all, Jessie remarked to him, "Well, Uncle Cade, your crop is ruined—you won't make anything. I thought my crop was hurt pretty badly, but not near as bad as yours; I declare you will not make bread and you will have to go to the poor house." The old man Cade replied, "You are a liar, sir; my crop is as good as yours, and I am not going to the poor house either." This is not all that was said, but is the pith of it, and shows pretty clearly what the old man was in this respect. Jessie knew him, and said what he did just to bring the old man out, and to hush up his complaints. John W. Bethea, the eldest son of old man Cade, married a Miss McLaurin; they had and raised four sons, Jessie, Laurin, Festus and Alonzo, and one daughter, at least, who became the second wife of Robert A. Brunson; they moved to North Carolina. Jessee, the oldest son of John W., married an Alabama lady; he died four or five years ago, at Dillon, and left his widow, two sons, Jessie and John, and two small daughters, Bessie and Lucile. John W. Bethea and wife are both dead. Evander R. Bethea, the second son of old Cade, married Mary Ann Stackhouse, and had one son, Jasper, and three daughters, Josephine, Carrie and Nannie, all of whom have already been noticed in or among the Stackhouse family. Laurin Bethea, the second son of John W. Bethea, married a Miss McLaurin, as I think; he is a farmer, and lives on Buck Swamp; know nothing of his family. "Fet" Bethea, the third son, married a Miss Stackhouse, daughter of the late Mastin C. Stackhouse; he died, leaving his widow with some children—the youngest of whom, a little girl, was taken by Rev. S. J. Bethea and wife, and they are raising it. Alonzo Bethea, the youngest son of John W. Bethea, is lost sight of; don't know whether he is living or dead, or whether he married or not—think, however, that he has emigrated to other parts, or is dead. Wm. C. Bethea, the third son of old man Cade Bethea, married Miss Virzilla Mace, a daughter of Moses and Drusilla Mace; they had two sons, Henry and John D., I think; they and their children have already been mentioned in or among the Mace family, to which reference is made. Calvin C. Bethea, the fourth son of old man Cade, married Miss Caroline Bethea, a daughter of "Creek Jessie;" they had one child, a son, named Jessie; the father, Calvin, was subjcet to epileptic fits, and on one occasion, while crossing a branch on Sweat Swamp, as supposed, an epileptic fit struck him and he fell in the water and was drowned; some years after his death, his widow, with her son, went to Texas; the son is grown, and the report is that they are doing well in that far off State. Henry, the fifth and youngest son of old man Cade Bethea, never married; he was killed or died in the war. Of the daughters of old Cade Bethea, the eldest, Caroline, a highly accomplished lady, as it was said, married James DuPre, of Marlborough County; she died childless, in about a year after her marriage. Harriet, the second daughter, married James McLaurin, of North Carolina; a few years back, they bought land on Buck Swamp and moved to it; think they are both dead—know nothing of their family. Mary Ann, the youngest daughter, married T. F. Stackhouse, and is dead, leaving him surviving; they have already been noticed in or among the Stackhouse family, to which reference is made. Not one of old man Cade Bethea's immediate family now survives.

Of the "Cape Fear set," Tristram, a son of old "English John," settled on Cape Fear River, N. C.; he had sons, James, Jessee, Elisha and William. Of these, Jessee, had Jessee, Simeon, David and Jessee (it seems two sons were named Jessee); Simeon had Reddick, Jessee, William and Philip; and Jessee, the elder, had Thomas, Tristram and John—this Tristram was the "Floral College" Tristram; and Jessee, the younger, had

John, Tristram, David and Jessee; and this latter Tristram had Jessee and Noah. William, the son of old Tristram, the "Cape Fear" settler, had John and William. Of these latter, John had William, John L., Jessee, David and Alexander; and William had David, John and Philip. The "Floral College" Tristram had Jessee, Daniel, Tristram, John and Thomas. Of these latter, all of them died without offspring. The eldest of these, Jessee, was well known in Marion; he was a graduate of the South Carolina College; studied law, settled in Marion to practice his profession, was a partner of the writer, as Sellers & Bethea, for several years; left Marion, abandoned the practice, never married, and died; he was a good lawyer, but too modest and diffident to enter into the "rough and tumble" of the Court House—he was a good office lawyer; after leaving Marion, he went to Marlborough and died there. This disposes of the "Cape Fear set" of Betheas—at least, as far as known.

Referring, again, to the "Sweat Swamp" set—old William had four sons, John, Goodman, Philip and Jessee—I think, all these have been noticed except, perhaps, Goodman. Goodman had two sons, Philip and Jessee, and the latter, Philip, had Goodman, William and Philip. Of the grand-daughters of "Sweat Swamp" William, Elizabeth married Jeremiah Walters, and raised a large family. Sarah married Timothy Rogers, a nephew of "Buck Swamp" John, and raised a large family. Pattie married John Braddy, and was the mother of the Braddys and their descendants, as have been and are now known in the county.

The writer may have inadvertently omitted some of this numerous and extensive family as laid down on the chart kindly furnished him, but do not think I have. From the original stock, "Old English John," it runs down to and includes the seventh and in one instance the eighth generation among the males bearing the name, and it is not improbable that among the females (if they had been given and traced), it would extend to and include the ninth and tenth generations, as it is a well known fact, that females generally marry younger than males, and consequently propagate faster than through the male line. If every family had a chart or tree like this, it would be an acquisition to the history of our people. It is a fact, that many of our people are shamefully ignorant as to their ancestry. It is a fact, that the writer has found in his inquiries on the subject among the people of Marion County, a few instances where the party inquired of did not know, and could not tell, who his grand-father was, and to his great surprise he has found it of men otherwise intelligent, and well posted in other matters. A chart, like that of the Betheas, in every family would forever dissipate such ignorance, and would enable every man to tell, at a word, whether he descended by natural and generic processes from his own species, or evoluted from a tadpole or a monkey. The Bethea chart is so constructed as to be indefinitely extended *ad infinitum* to the remotest generations.

Made in the USA
Monee, IL
25 February 2025

12962911R00020